The
Newport Medieval SI

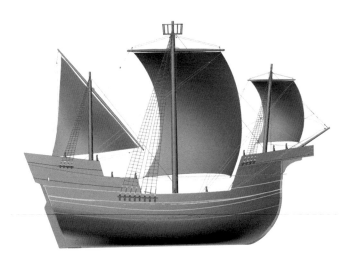

A Guide to the Discovery and Preservation of
a 15th Century Merchant Ship

Published by: The Friends of the Newport Ship ©
Newport, South Wales

2017
Reprinted 2018

ISBN No.   978-0-9519136-7-3

Front cover: "Final Resting Place"
A painting by David Jordan showing the Newport Ship

Contents

Dedication

Kate Hunter

The Friends of the Newport Ship dedicate this guide to Kate Hunter who died in January 2010. Kate was the real unsung hero of the project. She was the Conservator for Newport Museum and among other duties had been responsible for the conservation of a Romano-Celtic boat from Barland's Farm near Newport. After the recovery of the Newport Ship she was appointed Project Leader of the ship, and continued to be the driving force behind the project until her retirement due to ill health. She saw the project through many difficult stages and was, for a crucial period, an expert voice within the City Council able to advise on what was really needed to recover the ship. It was her abilities and enthusiasm that involved so many people in the project and helped raise the considerable funds needed to enable the project to succeed.

Councillor Charles Ferris
Patron of the Friends of the Newport Ship

Introduction: Medieval Trade

The Newport Medieval Ship is a unique historical artefact that was found buried in the mud of the River Usk in June 2002. It is the most complete fifteenth century merchant vessel ever unearthed, and its discovery has greatly contributed to our knowledge of late-medieval ships and seafaring. Years of research has revealed that she was probably built in the Basque Country, now split between France and Spain. Active from about 1449 to 1469, she carried a diverse medley of goods between Britain and Iberia during unstable times.

The fifteenth century stands at a cross-roads between historical eras. Many of the unmistakable characteristics of medieval life were still prominent: guilds and trade leagues, castles and royal courts. But this was also the early Renaissance: a time of accelerated advances. Few areas of life were left unchanged. The economy, in particular, was transformed in part by the leaps and bounds made in the art of shipbuilding.

For much of the medieval era there was a clear division between north and south in European shipbuilding styles. The dominant ship in northern waters was the cog (of which the Bremen Cog is the best surviving example). Unlike the longship type vessels which predated them, cogs had high sides and were powered entirely by a single sail. Mediterranean shipbuilders, on the other hand, continued to employ oar-power in the form of the galley, a long and narrow vessel that prevailed in southern Europe until the arrival of multi-masted carracks in the fifteenth century.

It is at this point that the northern and southern shipbuilding traditions began to converge and the Newport Ship is a product of this convergence. Its overall design is consistent with the carracks developed by the Iberian empires, yet the planking of the hull overlaps in a fashion usually found on northern ships. This meshing together of northern and southern influences is typical of Basque shipbuilding of the period.

The development of bigger, faster and more seaworthy ships facilitated greater international trade. One of the major routes made viable by these advances was that between Britain and Iberia, where the Newport Ship sailed.

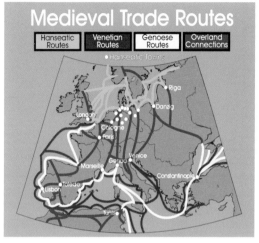

https://www.mydigitalchalkboard.org/portal/default/Resources/Viewer/ResourceViewer?action=2&resid=30767

The Anglo-Iberian trade route was established in the early twelfth century, but its expansion was not smooth. The Basque lands (and the trade of British merchants) tended to get caught up in the changing fortunes of Anglo-French warfare, with stability only improving after the Anglo-Castilian Treaty of 1466. This was a time of considerable uncertainty when, until the 1460s, Iberian ships had to purchase safe-passage in English waters.

Surviving records show that Basque ships became steadily more numerous in Anglo-Iberian trade during the fifteenth century, peaking slightly after the period when our ship was active. The main cargoes appear to have been wine and iron, but there are also references to large quantities of woad (mainly from the French city of Toulouse) being exported to Britain.

Some goods went in both directions depending on circumstances: examples are wheat (to relieve shortages) and wool (to meet the differing needs of spinners, dyers and weavers).

Many maps of medieval trade in western Europe show the route from Britain to the Mediterranean, but do not illustrate the route around the Brittany peninsula and into the Bay of Biscay. This was, however, an important route for both British and Basque merchants. Ports large and small along the Basque coast were bustling with merchant ships and our miraculous survivor was certainly one of them.

Bristol was the main recipient of Iberian trade with Britain. While mariners from other British ports mostly stuck to familiar routes, the men of Bristol proved more willing to explore new opportunities. The journey was long and arduous; a trip from Bristol to Lisbon could take three weeks, and was complicated further by the harsh waters of the Bay of Biscay. The ports of Fuenterrabia, Rentaria, Pasajes and San Sebastian provided the majority of Basque shipping to Bristol and it is likely that our ship was based (and maybe built) in one of these towns.

Trade from the Basque coast into Bristol expanded greatly during the second half of the fifteenth century and extended to ports as far north as Chester. So it may be that our ship was a frequent sight in the Bristol Channel and possibly the River Usk. At the end of her life she came to Newport for repairs, refit, or dismantling, and never left.

This guidebook tells the story of this extraordinary vessel – a find of international significance, and a treasure that must be preserved for years to come.

Medieval Newport

Newport in the fifteenth century was a small market town with a population of maybe 2,000 people. It stood on the west side of the River Usk, with a wooden bridge connecting it to the east side, and was divided by the Town Pill into the Great (north) Bailey and the Small (south) Bailey. The most imposing feature of the Great Bailey was the castle, a fourteenth century structure which acted as the administrative centre for the Lordship of Newport. This was one of the lordships created by England's military incursions into the Welsh Marches—and, as a result, the Lords of these territories enjoyed considerable independence from the King. Newport was a borough within the wider Lordship and in 1385 had been granted the right to hold a weekly market and an annual fair under a charter by Hugh, the second Earl of Stafford. A guild was also created to run the town's affairs.

The Small Bailey contained the town quay and the inlet in which the Newport Ship found its final resting place. There is some documentary evidence that the town had a stone wall, although nothing remains of this structure. A Murenger House was situated in the Small Bailey, a 'murenger' being someone with responsibility for the upkeep of a town's walls. The building now known as The Murenger House is probably post-medieval.

Newport was a relatively minor port in the fifteenth century. It was not a customs port and would have operated largely in Bristol's sphere of influence with many goods being transported there after arriving in Newport. However, the town did play a role in supplying castles like Raglan and Caerphilly, and the variable tide of the Usk meant the Pill (inlet) could serve as a natural drydock — ideal for repairing ships.

From 1469 until his death in 1471, the Lordship of Newport was in the possession of Richard Neville, the Earl of Warwick— known as 'the Kingmaker' for his role in deposing Henry VI from the throne in 1461 and then restoring him in 1470. After Neville was killed in the Battle of Barnet, control of Newport passed to the Duke of Gloucester, later King Richard III.

The World of the Newport Ship

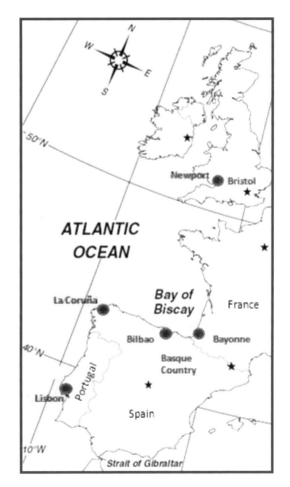

Sailing distances from Bristol

Bilbao - 580 Nautical Miles

La Coruña - 569 Nautical Miles

Lisbon - 992 Nautical Miles

Discovery and Excavation

In the early summer of 2002, along the banks of the River Usk, the Riverfront theatre and arts centre was under construction in the heart of Newport. Building work for the orchestra pit, stage, and auditorium required the lowering of a large steel cofferdam and many concrete piles into the ground. The Glamorgan-Gwent Archaeological Trust was given a watching brief over the site, and in early June it was handed over to a team of archaeologists for excavation.

Initial finds within the cofferdam included a timber-lined drain and a stone slipway, both post-medieval. Then, on 21 June 2002, the team began investigating some oak timbers which appeared along one of the proposed wall-lines. The alluvial clay in which the wood resided was cleared and more timbers became visible, revealing a series of posts connected by overlapping planks. Only gradually did it become apparent that the archaeologists had in fact chanced upon a find of international importance. The hull of a large ship was lying diagonally within the cofferdam, stretching from corner to corner.

The Newport Medieval Ship, as it came to be known, consists of 63 frame stations and over 2,000 timbers in total. Seventeen concrete piles had accidentally punctured the ship prior to excavation, with one of them having stabbed directly into the mast-step. The ship lay in a disfigured fashion – the starboard (right-hand) side had flattened out over the centuries, and at some point the port-side had been neatly cut, most likely to make way for a stone quay. The bow and stern, too, had been cut off by the cofferdam. Nevertheless, the visible section of the ship measured 22.5 metres in length and 7.65 metres in width.

Newport today

Newport circa 1450

From a painting by Anne Leaver

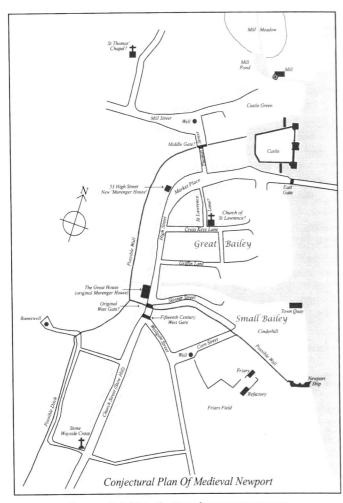

Conjectural Plan Of Medieval Newport

Plan prepared by Bob Trett with assistance from www.newportpast.com
The Newport Ship can be seen bottom right.

Newport's Riverfront Theatre and the plaque where it all began

The structure within
the cofferdam
Looking aft

The hull with most of the
framing removed
Looking aft

The ship, with its stern facing the Usk, was located in a former pill or inlet which seems to have been used as a natural dry-dock. A number of loose timbers were found laying on top of the vessel which, combined with the fact that only the lower hull remains, suggested that she was abandoned mid-way through dismantling. This helps explain what a ship of this size was doing in Newport. At first, the archaeologists operated under the assumption that only a select few timbers would be recorded and conserved, resulting in some loose timbers being discarded. But, after a vigorous "Save Our Ship" campaign and roadside vigil, the Welsh National Assembly announced on 23 August 2002 funding to the tune of £3.5 million for the full excavation of the ship. The option of lifting the vessel in a number of large sections was considered, but due to space limitations and the penetration of the hull by the concrete piles, it was ultimately decided to take the ship apart piece by piece in reverse order to its original construction. This was a time-consuming method – the initial excavation took over three months.

Archaeologists at work during the excavation

Separating the side-frames from the hull planking proved particularly problematic due to the remarkably well-preserved oak treenails which fastened them. Softwood wedges were inserted between the frames and the planks to allow access for saws, which lasted only a few days when cutting through the treenails. The corroded iron nails which connected each plank of the hull, on the other hand, were broken with ease. Once separated, each timber was attached to two or more slings and lifted out of the cofferdam by crane.

Some of the larger timbers had to be cut into sections. The keel which was formed from a single piece of beech wood measuring more than 20 metres long was cut into six parts; and the keelson (which runs parallel to the keel, inside the hull) was cut in two. On the 7th November, the keel was lifted and the main excavation phase was completed. Work continued on site in the following weeks, and large timbers were discovered which were thought to be shores onto which the ship had heeled over. This latter stage was completed in December 2002.

At this point in time, the recovery of the bows and stern became a major issue. The stern, in particular, would reveal a great deal about the ship – whether it had a transom (flat) stern or a pointed stern for instance. The rudder size, meanwhile, could reveal ship's approximate freight capacity. Mary Rose Archaeological Services were employed to ascertain the feasibility of recovering the bows and stern and in April 2003 Oxford Archaeology was contracted to recover as much as possible of these sections, both of which lay beyond the cofferdam. The bows and the stern-post were recovered, but the majority of the stern, if it remained, was deemed by Newport City Council to be too dangerous to excavate. The area where the stern might be was concreted over on 24th April as construction of the Riverfront arts centre resumed.

During the excavation, archaeologists made preliminary recordings of the timbers with each timber being given a unique code and its exact position on the ship defined. Photographic and photogrammetric surveys of the site and timbers were also taken at various stages.

Knee - CT1629
Weight 400 kg

The majority of the alluvial sediment, clay and luting or caulking (a sealant made of tar and animal fibre) was left on the timbers, to be cleaned at a later date.

In September 2002, the timbers began transportation to Llanwern Steelworks, where Corus (now Tata Steel) had offered a disused industrial unit for storage. There, they were placed in large fresh-water tanks where they could be kept temporarily until the long conservation process began.

Lifting the keelson

The Mast Step was penetrated by a concrete pile before the discovery of the ship

Frames and stringers (and a concrete pile)

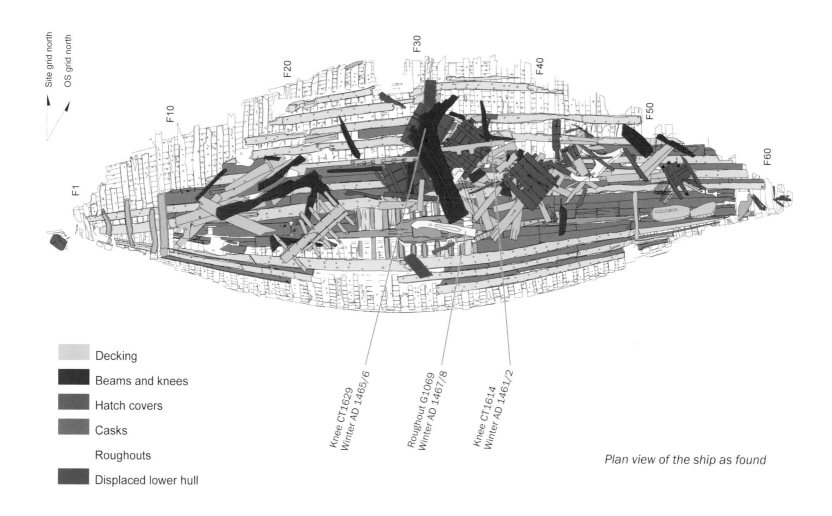

Site grid north

OS grid north

F1

F10

F20

F30

F40

F50

F60

Decking

Beams and knees

Hatch covers

Casks

Roughouts

Displaced lower hull

Knee CT1629
Winter AD 1465/6

Roughout G1069
Winter AD 1467/8

Knee CT1614
Winter AD 1461/2

Plan view of the ship as found

15

Recording and Conservation

Several thousand timbers (primarily oak), along with over 1000 small finds, were recovered during the excavations of 2002/3 in Newport. The intact hull was disassembled and raised, along with numerous disarticulated timbers. The timbers were housed in several different locations before a large unit on an industrial estate was set up to clean, record and conserve the timbers.

Concretions, tar, animal fibre and all visible corrosion products (primarily from the thousands of decayed wrought iron clench nails) were removed prior to recording the timbers.

Individual timbers were documented using FaroArm contact digitisers (human-operated articulated electronic coordinate

Timbers in the preservation tanks

measuring machines that can rapidly and accurately capture 3D (x,y,z) point data) and Rhinoceros3D computer aided design (CAD) software.

Accurate 3D digital wireframe drawings of each timber were created and included information such as edges, fasteners, wood grain and tool marks. The software had in-built tools that could quickly and accurately measure any distances between selected points within each 3D drawing. Additionally, networks of small stainless steel wood screws were inserted along the edges of the ship timbers. These reference points will stay in the material through conservation and possibly display.

The high-resolution 3D digital records of each hull timber were used to create digital solid models, which were, in turn, manufactured at 1:10 scale using a type of 3D printing called selective laser sintering. These miniature ship parts were then assembled into a model of the surviving hull form (page 18). This physical model has been used as the basis for the minimum and capital reconstruction efforts discussed later.

The majority of the hull timbers were cleaned and recorded between 2004 and 2008. Following initial documentation, a conservation condition assessment was carried out by the York Archaeological Trust, and the timbers were readied for conservation treatment. Timbers were initially soaked in a weak, 2% w/v, solution of tri-ammonium citrate to remove most soluble iron salts. This treatment was repeated until minimal iron salts were detected in the solution.

Timbers were thoroughly rinsed and then soaked in an increasingly concentrated solution of Polyethylene Glycol (PEG) 200 and 3350. Following impregnation by the PEG, batches of timbers were placed in a vacuum freeze drier for 2-4 months. The resulting timbers are stable and dry and are currently being housed in the ship centre in carefully controlled stores. Post-conservation analysis has shown that the hull planks are shrinking in a consistent fashion and trial reassembly efforts have provided evidence that the fasteners holes still line up.

Using the FARO Arm

Timbers going into a Freeze Drier

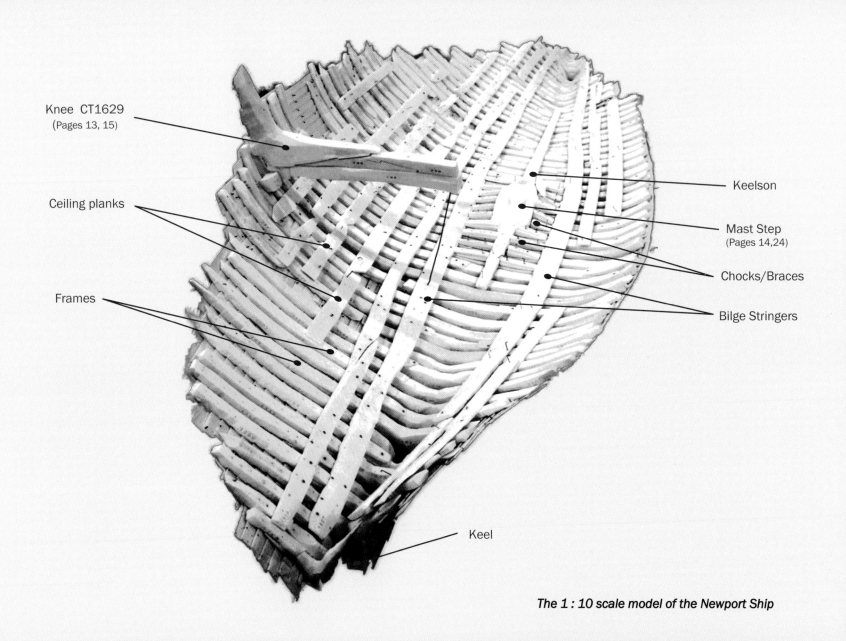

Knee CT1629
(Pages 13, 15)

Ceiling planks

Frames

Keelson

Mast Step
(Pages 14,24)

Chocks/Braces

Bilge Stringers

Keel

The 1 : 10 scale model of the Newport Ship

About the Ship

Origins

Although it was apparent from an early stage that the Newport Ship was a merchant vessel, her precise origins and dating remained unknown for many years after her discovery. Early estimations suggested she may have been a seventeenth-century craft, but that proved wide of the mark. The first accurate dating was provided while the ship was still being excavated by the examination of a large hanging knee. The tree from which it was cut was found to have been felled in South-West Britain during the winter of 1465-6. The method used to determine this is called dendrochronology, which involves measuring the annual growth-rings found on timbers and their comparison against established regional chronologies.

Although some of the planks from the Newport Ship were found to have come from British trees, having been added during repairs in or after 1459, most of them could not be matched against existing data in 2002. At that time, archaeologists had access to fairly comprehensive growth-ring chronologies for northern Europe, but very limited datasets for southern Europe. The fact that most of the wood could not be matched against any northern datasets provided the first indication that the ship was probably not British.

Tree rings

Another clue that the ship was foreign came while the timbers were being cleaned in 2006 when a small silver coin was found deliberately lodged between the keel and the stem post. Further examination revealed that the coin was a French *petit blanc* (small white), minted in the village of Cremieu, near Lyon, in 1447. It was placed there as a charm for good luck and divine protection, a practice established in the Roman era. This find contributed to early speculation that the ship was built along the Atlantic coast of France.

However, more recent research firmly suggests that the ship was built in the Basque Country, which lies on the border between modern Spain and France. Nigel Nayling, an archaeologist and timber specialist who has been involved with the ship since its excavation, collaborated with Basque dendrochronology experts to explore the possibility of the ship having Iberian origins. Once the growth-ring

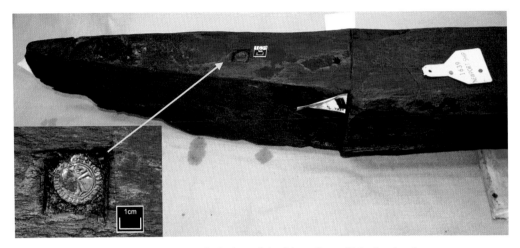

The petit blanc coin in its original location within the keel

work on 'the ship in Newport'. As the Basque ship arrived in the town around the time the letter was written, it could well be the ship mentioned by Neville. Kings and powerful nobles retained the right to commandeer ships for military purposes, so it is possible that this ship had come into the Kingmaker's possession.

chronologies in Iberia had been sufficiently expanded by 2011, a strong correlation was found against the Newport Ship's timbers which places them in the upland interior of the Basque Country. The trees were felled around 1449, and the ship would have been built soon after. As the Basque region did not have its own coinage at this time, it used Portuguese and French currency instead; hence the placement of a French coin in the keel.

Examination of the shores which supported the ship once it arrived in Newport revealed that the trees were cut in 1467/8, meaning the ship had a working life of about 20 years. It is still not clear, however, why a Basque ship would have come to Newport for refit, repairs, or dismantling.

One potential answer is found in a letter penned by Earl Richard Neville of Warwick, the so-called 'Kingmaker,' who was Lord of Newport at the time. The letter, written in 1469, appears to detail payment for repair

The petit blanc

*Sir Richard 'The King Maker' Neville,
16th Earl of Warwick (1428 - 1471)*

The "Warwick" Letter

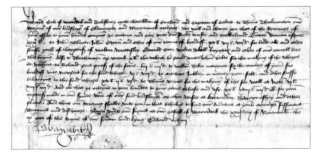

Letter reproduced with the
permission of the
Warwickshire County
Record Office
CR 1998/J2/177

Translation

Richard Earl of Warwick and Salisbury great Chamberlain of England and captain of Calais to Thomas Throckmorton our receiver of our lordship of Glamorgan and Morgannwyg greeting. We well (will) and charge you that of the revenues of your office to your hands coming you content and pay unto our right trusty and welbeloved Harry Vernan esquire £30 to John Blunte John Owen and other of our town of Cardiff £15 8s for bread, ale and other stuff parcel of the expenses of Walter Wrattisley, Edward Grea Walter Skull ? Knights and other of our council late there being also to Thrahawron (Traherne ?) ap Merik £10 the which he paid unto John Colt for **the making of the ship at Newport** to Richard Port purser of the same 53s 4d, to William Toker mariner for the carriage of iron from Cardiff unto Newport for the said ship 6s 8d to Matthew Jubber in money, iron, salt amd other stuff **belonging to the said ship** £15 2s 6d,to Thomas Veyne for the making of the sea wall at Neath £16 13s 4d and over that you retain in your hands to your own behoof and use £20 18s 4d for your expenses made in our service within ? Of our said lordships as other wise ar Camarthen, Swansea and other places. And thus our writing shall be unto you in that to behalve to fore our auditors at your accompt sufficient warrant and discharge. Given under our signet at our castle of Warwick the 22 day of November the ninth year of the reign of our sovereign lord king Edward the fourth. [**1469**]

R Warwyk

Construction

The Newport Ship was built in a long-standing technique established by the Vikings – known as clinker or lapstrake shipbuilding. This method is characterized primarily by a hull made with overlapping planks, as opposed to the carvel method in which the planks are placed edge-to-edge to provide a smooth finish.

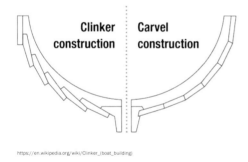

Clinker construction : **Carvel construction**

https://en.wikipedia.org/wiki/Clinker_(boat_building)

In the clinker tradition, the outer hull is constructed before the side-framing (or rib cage) is inserted. The hull of the Newport Ship was probably constructed in stages, with the bottom planking assembled first, then floor timbers, followed by more planking and eventually the side timbers, or futtocks. The side-frames were fastened to

A sample of clinker construction

the hull planking with oak treenails, which expand and seal the hole once they become wet. The planks, meanwhile, were connected to each other with thousands of wrought iron clench nails with iron roves.

Luting (or caulking), a mixture of tar and animal hairs, was laid down along the areas where planks overlap in order to make the hull water-tight.

Although there are some disadvantages to the clinker tradition, there are also considerable advantages that helped it survive in northern Europe and parts of southern Europe well into the Early Modern era.

Oak Treenail

A rove - the small iron plate that the nail passes through and is peened over

On the one hand, clinker hulls tend to be irregular and because each plank on a clinker-built ship is fastened to its neighbours, the only way to repair a crack is to add another plank (called a tingle) on the outside. However, the overlapping nature of clinker hulls allows for thinner and therefore lighter planks to be used. This also forgoes the sometimes lengthy sealing treatment required in the carvel tradition.

Apart from the keel, which was made from a single beech tree, the ship was made primarily from oak. The planks, most of which are three to four metres long, were crafted from radially-split logs (meaning they were split lengthwise via the insertion of wedges), and the resulting planks were smoothed out using axes and adzes.

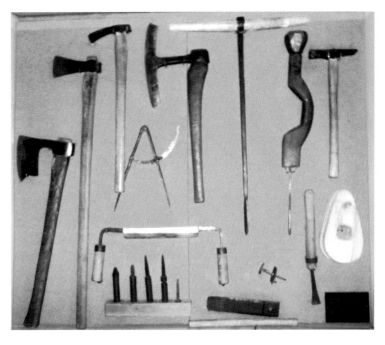

Replica 15th Century tools as would have been used by the builders of the Newport Ship

Damage and possible refitting

The ship was found in a substantially damaged state. Extra pumps were installed later in her life, suggesting the crew may have been confronted with a growing number of cracks and leaks. The most noteworthy bit of damage was the deep crack in the mast-step (see page 24).

The present theory is that the ship was initially brought to Newport for refitting work, which involved adding additional timbers to the upper section of the vessel and possibly installing an extra deck. During this process, however, the cradle supporting the ship in its pill collapsed. The ship was flooded during successive tides, and after attempts to drain the vessel failed the decision was made to dismantle and salvage as much as possible. Once abandoned, the ship seems to have been used as a rubbish skip.

The mast step showing the split in the keelson

Many of the components that were removed during dismantling, including the main mast, would have been sold or reused.

While in Newport the ship was propped up using large timber shores, and a doorway was cut into its starboard side to allow easy access for workers. The starboard shores collapsed at some point, and the weight of the mud which gathered over the ship in the following centuries resulted in the starboard side flattening out, creating an asymmetric shape.

The Ship's pumps

A total of four pump locations were found in the hull of the vessel, along with some pump components. Water was sent through hollowed-out trunks by leather burr valves (right). The ship's pumps pre-date all known comparisons.

A crudely-cut pump hole near the stern of the ship suggests an extra pump was hurriedly added later in the ship's life.

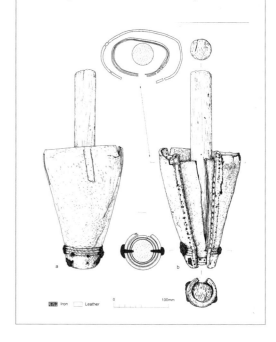

The midships pump basket

Cargo

Numerous components from storage containers were recovered from the excavation site, suggesting that the Newport Ship carried its varied cargo in an assortment of barrels and casks. Hundreds of triangular wooden chocks were also found, which were possibly used to hold the barrels steady during voyages. Dunnage was also used to secure goods in place.

Many of the barrel timbers bear unique merchants' markings which acted like signatures and identified each barrel as belonging to a particular trader. These markings would be highly useful when trying to recover stolen goods.

Wine was a major British import from Iberia and likely comprised part of the ship's cargo, along with iron. Grain was also traded back and forth depending on harvests. The consumables found within the ship included a wide range of nuts, fruits, and livestock. Dried fish seems to have been one of the ship's staple goods, with species ranging from cod and salmon to flatfish and small shark. Some of this, however, would have been intended for consumption by the crew rather than for trade.

Any ship that carries so much food is vulnerable to infestation. An ample assortment of pest remains were discovered within the confines of the ship; rats, flies, wood-worms, beetles, and weevils among them, along with some species never before found in the UK. Some of the recovered animal bones have bite-marks on them, suggesting that a dog was kept for pest-control.

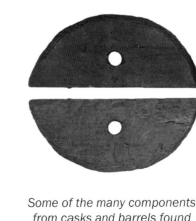

Some of the many components from casks and barrels found on the ship

Estimated Ship's Particulars

Length Overall	30.6 m
Length on loaded waterline	27.0 m
Length of keel	21.6 m
Beam	8.9 m
Draft (loaded)	3.9 m (3.5 m Forward)
Freeboard	2.5 m
Sail area - Main	254.6 sq. m
Fore	63.6 sq. m
Mizzen	76.5 sq. m
. Total	394,7 sq. m
Displacement (Loaded)	392.5 tons
Lightship	131.5 tons (hull and rigging)
Deadweight	261.0 tons (cargo, ballast, crew and provisions)
Weight of ballast	74.0 tons
Weight of cargo	174.5 tons
Internal volume	996.0 cu. m
Volume for cargo	225.0 cu. m
Stowage factor	1.3 cu. m / ton

The Ship with a typical cargo

Performance

Maximum based on an assumed 50% sail efficiency and a clean smooth hull.

In reality achieving 75% of the maximum would be optimistic and 50 - 60 % would be typical.

	Upwind	Reach	Downwind
Apparent sail area	221 sq, m	395 sq. m	255 sq. m
Wind Force 3	4.3 knots	5.4 knots	4.6 knots
Wind Force 4	4.9 knots	6.1 knots	5.2 knots
Wind Force 5	6.2 knots	7.6 knots	6.5 knots

Visualising the Newport Ship

2002

There is a multifarious range of sources from which we can draw a general picture of medieval shipbuilding: manuscripts, medieval books and maps, academic publications, specialist modern books and museums. When it comes to the construction and appearance of a specific vessel, however, archaeologists must examine the existing structure before turning to external sources.

Working towards an accurate depiction of the Newport Ship has been a long journey. In the initial enthusiasm following its discovery, several paintings and drawings appeared from local artists aiming to provide a rough visualization of the ship. Among the best was that of Paul Deacon, as shown here.

It shows a single-masted ship with a centre line rudder on a curved stern, along with a simple stern castle; but without the forecastle (foc'sle) that such vessels might need to traverse the open Atlantic.

It also lacks a foremast and mizzen mast to assist with the steering of the vessel. Although this depiction helped to attract public interest in the ship, the research carried out since 2002 suggests it looked rather different.

Paul Deacon's illustration of the ship, with Newport Castle in the background (2002)

2003 - 2009

A more accurate rendition was produced by marine historian Owain Roberts in 2003. He assumed that such a large vessel would have had three masts and a definite forecastle, plus a sterncastle/quarterdeck. Ships showing these features are illustrated in various books and manuscripts from the early and middle years of the 15th Century. The larger central sail was the primary means of propulsion. The sails on the smaller fore mast and mizzen mast helped steer the ship; though they may also have increased the speed slightly.

In 2009, visualizations of the ship took another leap forward as a result of the digitalisation of the timbers. This involved the recording of around 2,000 timbers and smaller artefacts using FARO arm technology (see pages 16-17), and facilitated the development of more accurate reconstructions. The examination of the timbers is a continuous process and has produced multiple evolving interpretations of the ship.

Three-masted iteration of the ship by Owain Roberts (2003)

Pat Tanner's minimalist reconstruction (2013)

2012-2014

In 2012-2014, Pat Tanner produced a range of illustrations based on both a 'minimum' and a 'capital' reconstruction of the vessel. The minimum reconstruction, shown here, is based strictly on the archaeological evidence, and as such is limited by the incomplete nature of the recovered ship. Together with the transom (flat) stern, the most notable feature of this version is that it shows only one deck. Medieval iconography, however, suggests that vessels the size of the Newport Ship typically had at least two decks.

The capital reconstruction, on the other hand, brings in parallel archaeological evidence to display what the ship probably looked like. For example, consideration of the ship's regular trading route from the Iberian peninsula to the Bristol Channel area and the illustrations of such vessels shown in medieval books and manuscripts resulted in the revised reconstruction shown on page 30.

The lower hull on the capital reconstruction is exactly the same as that shown in the minimum reconstruction. However, the use of contextual evidence gave the ship an extra deck and a more formidable forecastle and stern castle/quarter deck. The colour scheme divides up the various sections of the complete ship as follows:

- BROWN for the surviving timbers of the Ship.
- BLUE for the minimum elements needed for a watertight hull.
- DARK GREEN for the lower deck.
- LIME for the upper deck
- RED for elements for which there is no physical evidence, but which must have been present given the ship's size and time period.

These changes produce a stronger, higher and more seaworthy vessel capable of repeated voyages along the Atlantic coasts of Europe.

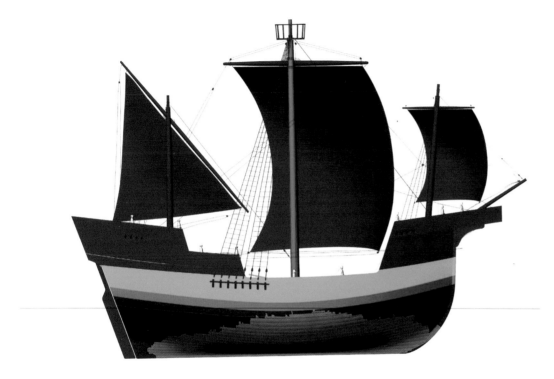

Pat Tanner's capital reconstruction (2014)

2014

In 2014 a portrayal of the ship was produced by Peter Power (see page 32), a marine artist who has also produced well-known depictions of the Mary Rose.

The ship in Peter Power's painting has a lot in common with typical sixteenth century carracks. Two prominent wooden wales* run along the side of the ship to give greater strength to the hull. The use of carvel construction would be needed to allow gun ports, so Power speculated that the upper hull might have been made in the carvel style. However, although interesting, these conjectures are not supported by the weight of available evidence.

* wale - a thick strake or belt of planking along the sides of a vessel to stiffen the hull

2017

A continuing programme of research in Newport, Lampeter, Cork and the Basque Country has allowed a process of 'filling in' with reasonable certainty the details of the ship's appearance.

The latest and most accurate painting (see page 33) is by David Jordan and was given to the Ship Project in January 2017. Jordan chose to represent the vessel at the end of her days, with Newport castle shown prominently in the background. Unlike the Peter Power illustration, Jordan's presentation of the ship depicts it built entirely in the clinker style, in line with the Project's opinion on the matter, and the hull is black due to it being covered in tar. The ship is shown to have two decks along with prominent fore and stern castles.

Emptied of cargo, fittings and ballast, and with yard arms removed to further reduce weight, the ship is about to be towed by horses into the pill where she will remain for over five centuries. It is uncertain whether horses or oxen were used to pull the ship into its resting place, but it is a compelling possibility.

An alternative would have been to use large capstans mounted at the inner end of the pill and possibly worked by members of the crew.

The ship reconstructed by Tanner and painted by Jordan bears very little resemblance to that shown by Paul Deacon in 2002, demonstrating the fruits of over a decade of analysis. And it is likely that further research will give cause to challenge present theories. In this sense, the ship is a piece of living history.

"The Newport Medieval Ship" by Peter Power

"The Final Resting Place" by David Jordan

Life on Board

Substantial three-masted vessels like the Newport Ship required a crew of around 30-50 men to operate the complex system of rigging and cordage. This resourceful team of merchant sailors forged a career out of navigating treacherous waters during a politically volatile period in European history. Britain and Iberia were both rocked by a long series of conflicts and fallouts, while the busy Atlantic trade routes were infested with opportunistic pirates. Yet life must go on – and so it did for the crew of this ship. Although most of the ship's valuables were removed during her partial dismantling, the artefacts excavated with the hull still give us a fascinating insight into daily life on board this vessel.

Activities

Entertainment was crucial on the long journeys between Britain and Iberia, and board-games provided some welcome relief. A finely-carved boxwood game piece was uncovered, measuring 33mm across, which was likely used as a multi-purpose piece in games like nine men's morris and early versions of backgammon.

Decorated boxwood game piece

Some wooden tools were also excavated such as a 100mm awl or fid and a knife handle – along with remnants of the iron blade and small rivets. Such tools would have been necessary for the ongoing repairs of equipment and clothing.

Wooden awl, likely used to craft and repair leather items

Knife handle

Clothing

The limited textile fragments found on the ship are mostly formed of undyed wool, woven in a twill or tabby pattern into heavy and rough work clothing.

Rough textile fragments

Much more was unearthed in the way of footwear: a total of eight leather shoes and three boots, albeit with no matching pairs. The most noticeable of the five distinct styles found is the highly fashionable 'poulaine,' which has a pointed toe filled with moss to hold its shape. Interestingly, the poulaine shoes found on the Newport Ship exceed medieval laws regarding toe-length by over an inch.

'Poulaine' shoe with a pointed toe

Life at sea required efficient and clever re-use of old resources, including worn-out clothes. Textile clothing, once beyond repair, was often put to use plugging leaks in the hull, while the leather from the upper part of a damaged boot could be refashioned into a shoe. It is possible that many of the leather fragments on the ship originally came from footwear.

Diet

Salted fish and meat formed the basis of most medieval crews' provisions, and it was likely the same for those on board the Newport Ship. This was probably supplemented by some of the other durable foods recovered, including nuts, grapes, apples, peaches, shellfish, and oysters. The presence of livestock bones on the ship indicates that animals were slaughtered during voyages, while fresh fish would also have been caught and eaten while at sea.

The bone remains reveal some intimate details about the lives of those on board – for instance, the cut marks are consistent with the butcher being right-handed. Other artefacts were found which have relevance to consumption habits; namely, an ash-wood bowl (with what may be ownership markings underneath) and hundreds of pottery fragments from jugs, pitchers, jars, and lids. Most of this pottery was Portuguese micaceous red-ware. Showing numerous signs of wear and tear, these items would have been intended for use by the crew.

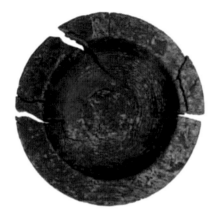

Wooden bowl with possible ownership markings underneath

Navigation and Sailing

Only one item was found which relates to navigation; a murky sandglass fragment that was located near the mast-step. Sandglasses like this were fitted inside wooden frames and, together with pivoted compasses and portolan charts, formed the backbone of medieval navigation. Time-keeping was necessary to track progress along a plotted course, although medieval ships tended to stay within sight of land.

Hygiene

With livestock and pests aplenty, as well as a hull plugged with tar, the smell on board the Newport Ship would not have been pleasant. Making matters worse for the sailors, head lice and fleas were commonplace. Both human and animal fleas were discovered in the bilge of the ship.

Two wooden combs were found – one single-sided and one double-sided. The finer teeth on the double-sided comb were used to remove lice, while the thicker teeth would have been used for general grooming.

Double-sided comb

Sandglass

Meanwhile, the fifteenth century witnessed great strides in sailing technology as single-masted vessels gradually gave way to two or three-masted ships. This naturally required a greater volume of cordage and rigging equipment, and the Newport Ship provided archaeologists with a healthy array of these fittings. Both hemp and grass rope were recovered, ranging from 38mm to 125mm in circumference, along with a wide variety of rigging components. Heart blocks, pendant blocks, parrel trucks, and lifting hooks were among the excavated parts that would have been used to manoeuvre this formidable ship.

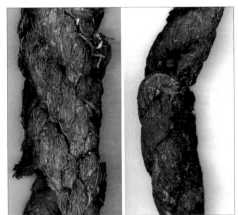

Grass hawser   *Hemp rope*

Heart block

Conflict

Piracy and privateering was rife in the late medieval era. Kings and nobles encouraged their merchants to attack the trade vessels of rival monarchs, and there were no laws governing violence at sea until Henry V's Statute of the Truces in 1414. A brief period of comparative calm followed, but piracy resurged under the reign of Henry VI (1422-1461), and it is in this context that the Newport Ship operated.

The danger did not end where dry land begins; even ports were hazardous places that often came under attack by rival fleets. The ports of northern Iberia, where the Newport Ship probably called, were favoured targets for English pillaging – although Bristol would have provided something of a safe-haven from French attacks. The Bay of Biscay became particularly chaotic following the fall of Gascony to the French in 1453, which plunged England's wine trade into a state of disarray. All in all, the Atlantic trade routes were fraught with peril.

Merchant vessels therefore had to carry martial equipment for their own protection. To this end, the Newport Ship possessed stone shot of various sizes, and therefore had several guns. Stone shot shatters when fired, inflicting maximum damage to human targets while leaving the opposing ship relatively unharmed and ready for the taking. Whether this ship was ever involved in its own piratical activities is a matter for conjecture, but a capacity for retaliation was an inescapable requirement of medieval seafaring.

Stone shot of various sizes

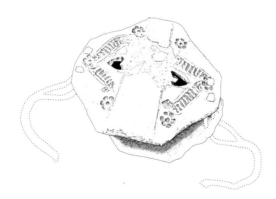

Decorated archer's wrist-guard

An archer's wrist guard was also found, bearing intricate decorations and inscribed with the Latin word *amilla*, or bracer. Perhaps most intriguing, however, are the fragments of a decorated iron helmet. Running along the helmet's rim are Gothic Latin letters quoting a Biblical passage from Luke, 4:30, which reads: 'But Jesus passing through the midst of them went on his way.' This passage was used as a safety charm and has been found on multiple armour pieces from the period.

Decorated brass helmet piece

Trade

As ships became bigger throughout the late-Medieval era, they spent more and more time loading and unloading in ports. The increased freight capacity of merchant vessels, along with a recovery of population after the Black Death in the fourteenth century, catalysed a boom in overseas trade. This, in turn, spurred the growth of seaports like Bristol, where the Newport Ship probably traded.

Other than the French petit blanc found placed within the keel, four other coins were dug up. All of these represent Portuguese copper currency. Three of them are *ceitils* minted during the reign of King Afonso V, which spanned nearly half a century from 1438 to 1481, while the final coin is a *real preto* from the time of King Duarte I (1433-1438). Although these coins were not formally part of the British currency system, a fair number have been found in Wales and South West England.

Trade and accounting was aided by the use of jettons, or counters. Like many others from the period, the decorated brass jetton found on the Newport Ship (top left in the image above) was made in Nuremberg, Germany. It carries an image of what may be a crowned head, obscured somewhat by a sizeable fold.

Jetton (top left) and 4 Portuguese coins

Merchants Marks

Merchants' marks were very common between about 1400 and 1700. In the Middle Ages there was a great risk of shipwreck or piracy, and individual traders were careful to put only a small consignment of goods in any one ship. By carrying their goods in several ships they reduced the chance of losing an entire stock. Therefore it was important that they could easily identify their own goods from the goods of other merchants, and they did this by having their own distinct personal marks, like a present day logo.

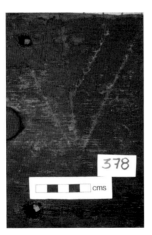

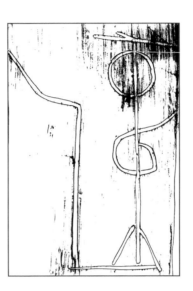

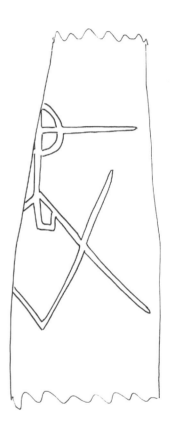

Some Merchants Marks discovered on timbers associated with the Newport Ship

History of the Friends of the Newport Ship (FoNS)

By Jean Gray

July 2002

Substantial remains of a ship are uncovered during the building of the Riverfront Theatre and Arts Centre.

Newport City Council announces plans to bury the remains of the ship after a brief excavation and retrieve only 10–15% of the timber for scientific analysis.

16th August 2002

Save Our Ship (SOS) campaign launched.

17th August 2002

- A 24/7 vigil at the site began.
- A petition started, collecting 6,000 signatures in 6 days.
- Media involvement - Press – BBC – ITV.
- Letters sent to prominent figures at Newport City Council, Welsh Assembly, MP's and Cadw
- The Council for British Archaeology allows FoNS a page on their website giving worldwide publicity.

21st August 2002

- A flotilla of boats from Uskmouth Sailing Club and other river users sailed up to the site. Many hundreds came to line the river banks . A great evening.

23rd August 2002

Plan to give £3.5m for full excavation and recording is announced . To be funded by the Welsh Assembly, Newport City Council and Cadw.

The 6,000+ petition presented to Jenny Randerson AM, Culture Secretary for the Welsh Assembly.

25th August 2002

Activists agree to continue SOS as "Support Our Ship" and "Friends of the Newport Ship" was formed.

- To promote knowledge and information about the Newport Medieval Ship
- To foster an appreciation of the maritime and industrial heritage of South Wales
- To provide a forum for debate
- To monitor progress on conservation
- To contribute to the promotion of Newport's rich heritage.

The updated constitution can be viewed on the FoNS website. *www.newportship.org* Over the last 15 years membership has remained between 400-800.

2005

Charitable status granted

Our activities are many and varied.

We produce and distribute books, leaflets and flyers to spread the word about the Ship.

We have attended hundreds of events with our displays and merchandise.

A varied range of merchandise has been produced to raise funds and awareness of The Newport Ship.

From the funds generated by membership, sales and donations, approx. £50,000 has been given to support the project.

Open Days and guided tours are arranged and we have hosted many groups on visits to the Newport Ship Centre.

At the Excavation

Looking Forward

by Philip Cox, Chairman of the Friends of the Newport Ship

At the time of writing this edition of the new Guide Book, we are entering 2017 and looking forward to celebrating the 15th Anniversary of the finding of the Ship. Time has passed so quickly, so much has been done but there remains lot yet to do.

We have over 50% of the timbers back in our conservation store, and the remainder will be returned to us ready for reassembly before the end of 2018. All we need is somewhere in which our mighty ship can be put back together.

Newport City Council is working on a plan. Officers have identified their preferred location on the 3rd floor of Newport Museum and Art Gallery and the adjacent former Reference Library and are ensuring that the building is structurally fit-for-purpose and can provide the environment that is needed for the ongoing care of the ship. Nothing has been found that rules the building out as a possible candidate as a future home for the ship.

We are all awaiting the engineer's report that is required to identify necessary modifications to the space – take out a roof-supporting column and increase the available height to ensure that the reassembled ship will fit, along with all the other items that we want to see displayed – including the Barland's Farm romano-celtic boat that languishes away from public view in our timber store!

In the meantime, plans are progressing with regard to the reassembly itself. Ongoing work is confirming that the conserved timbers will all still fit together and other work is experimenting with the fixings and supports required as part of the reassembly. This section is currently on display in the extended conservation store at the Medieval Ship Centre.

The actual design of the cradle in which the reassembled ship will rest will be designed in collaboration with Swansea University, part funded by the Friends of Newport Ship.

The big question that visitors ask is 'will we rebuild the rest of the ship as well?' … and the answer is no we will not! The main reason behind this is that the original timbers are not as strong as they were when they were built and they now would not support the physical weight of the rest of the vessel. Also, the complete ship would require much more space to display.

As an alternative, we are experimenting with digital imagery. Using this technology, we can 'paint in' the remaining parts of the ship without regard to the confines of space. Other elements of this will provide further opportunities to explore the ship internally and externally within virtual reality.

As ever, the big issue is funding. The Heritage Lottery Fund is collaborating with the Council and are being supportive, and proposing a funding plan. This does however leave a sizeable sum to be found either from the public purse, or from other grant giving bodies, corporate sponsors and private contributions.

The Friends of Newport Ship will continue to support the project in whatever role is required. We currently seek to:

- raise and maintain public awareness through the opening of the Medieval Ship Centre on a regular basis (currently every Friday and Saturday from Easter until the end of October)

- increase footfall at the Medieval Ship Centre through encouraging organised visits

- produce this guide book, newsletters, leaflets, and articles in relevant publications

- find new audiences: visiting suitably themed public events with our travelling exhibition

- give talks and lectures about the project and the future plans for the reconstruction and display of the ship

- Maintain the Medieval Ship Centre and updating, improving and expanding the displays to encourage visitors to visit again and see what's new

- Expanding the work of FoNS to bring Medieval Studies to a wider audience (including schools)

- support the project financially by buying essential equipment and services, getting grants and making donations which help secure other funding

- provide volunteer guides and additional activities for public open days and other visits to the Ship Centre

- help with the archaeological and conservation work.

The active members of the Friends have contributed thousands of hours of voluntary work, but even members who can't assist directly provide vital support. Merely by joining they help demonstrate the level of public interest in the ship. That's vital as we seek donations, sponsorship, grants and to get commitment to complete the project. All Friends are kept up to date with a bi-monthly newsletter and an annual update, and have the opportunity to attend lectures and other events at the Medieval Ship Centre.

All this continues to need support – your support, and the support of many more, those that we can encourage to join the Friends, to volunteer to help at the Ship Centre and out and about at events, to give freely of their time (for which we are incredibly grateful) and to bring our hopes and dreams towards reality.

2002 *"Usk Treasure" by John Stiles*

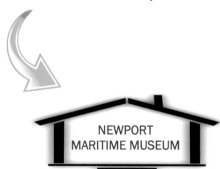

Some Other Preserved Vessels

Vasa
Stockholm, Sweden
Built 1626-1628 and sunk 1628
Raised 1961
www.vasamuseet.se

Mary Rose
Portsmouth
Built 1510
Sunk 1545
Raised 1982
www.maryrose.org

Fram
Oslo, Norway
Built 1893
Preserved 1936
www.frammuseum.no

Cutty Sark
Greenwich, London
Built 1869
www.rmg,co,uk

Bremen Cog
Bremen, Germany
Built c.1380
Found 1962
www.dsm.museum

Viking Ships
Oslo, Norway and Roskilde, Denmark
Late 8th Century to mid 11th Century
www.khm.uio.no
www.vikingskibsmuseet.dk

Barlands Farm Boat
Severn Estuary
Romano Celtic
Found 1993
Presently stored at Newport Medieval
Ship Centre